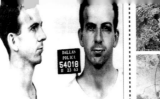

Picture Credits
t=top, tr=top right, tl=top left, b=bottom, bl=bottom left, br=bottom right, m=middle, ml=middle left, mr=middle right

P6: Gerard Richardson (mr); P9: Adam L. Clevenger (m); P9: Annie Dalbéra (bl); P9: Jefry Lagrange Reyes (br); P14: John Trumbull (tr); P15: Mwanner (b); P17: EncMstr (br); P17: Matt Kozlowski (br); P18: Kevin Myers (bl); P26: UpstateNYer (l); P36: Smile Lee (mr); P39: goodvint (br); P40: Rmhermen (tl); P41: John Morse (mr)

PAB-0912-0156

ISBN: 978-1-4867-1398-1

Fact Checker:
Jay Johnson

Written by
Dan Carpenter
Sean Kennelly

TABLE OF CONTENTS

D.Y.K.A.

DO YOU KNOW ABOUT...

How much do you know about the story of America? Find awesome facts throughout the book as you learn more about our great nation. Just look for the D.Y.K.A. symbol!

AMERICA THE INCREDIBLE

The story of America is an incredible tale involving thousands of fascinating people and events. You can spend a lifetime learning about the stories that make up the history of the United States. Here are just a few of those episodes.

SOUTHERN CHIVALRY — ARGUMENT versus CLUB'S.

D.Y.K.A. In the tense days before the outbreak of the Civil War, a US senator from Massachusetts was nearly beaten to death by a congressman from South Carolina in the Capitol building in Washington, DC. Why? The two men were arguing over the issue of **slavery**.

D.Y.K.A. During World War II, John F. Kennedy's ship, *PT-109*, was sliced in half by a Japanese destroyer in the Pacific. He and eleven of his crewmen swam to a deserted island. They were rescued when native islanders discovered them and took a message that Kennedy had scratched into a coconut shell to a nearby Allied base.

D.Y.K.A. In December 1773, colonists threw 96,000 pounds of tea into Boston Harbor. They called it the Boston Tea Party. However, tea does not mix well with cold water. It is also very light, so it floated in piles on top of the water. Dunes of tea spread over Boston Harbor for many days after the event. The British Government's angry reaction to the Tea Party led to the American Revolution.

D.Y.K.A. Confederate General Robert E. Lee's secret plans for the Battle of Antietam (September 1862) fell into enemy hands when a Union soldier from Indiana found the plans wrapped around three large cigars. The Battle of Antietam was a draw and was the bloodiest single day in US history.

BATTLE OF ANTIETAM.

D.Y.K.A. In 1936, the Summer Olympic games were held in Berlin, Germany. Sadly, Germany was under the control of the ruthless **dictator** Adolf Hitler at that time. Hitler was a **racist** and wanted to use the Olympic games to show the world that Germans were superior to other races. However, African-American sprinter Jesse Owens dominated the games. He won four gold medals, which was more than any other athlete at the games.

D.Y.K.A. A massive riot broke out at the University of Mississippi in 1962 when students learned that a black man was attempting to enroll at the school. Two people died in the violence before troops from the 82nd Airborne arrived in the middle of the night to take control of the campus.

D.Y.K.A. Teddy Roosevelt was shot in the chest just minutes before he was to give a campaign speech in 1912. He said, "I give you my word, I do not care a rap about being shot; not a rap," and he addressed the gathered crowd for ninety minutes before allowing himself to be taken to the hospital.

D.Y.K.A. In 1961, President John F. Kennedy showed the world the power of American dreams when he announced the goal of landing a man on the moon by the end of the 1960s. On July 20, 1969, that dream came true when US astronaut Neil Armstrong set foot on the moon. "That's one small step for man, one giant leap for mankind," said Neil Armstrong.

D.Y.K.A. The second-deadliest event in US history is not as well-known as the Civil War; it is the **influenza** epidemic of 1918. An estimated 650,000 Americans died in the last four months of that year. Society nearly came to a halt as Americans were terrified to shake hands or even be near one another.

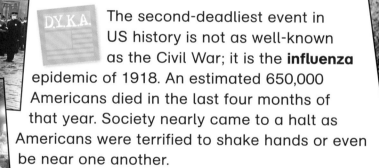

D.Y.K.A. Though there were other railroads around the world, America's transcontinental railroad remains one of the most amazing accomplishments ever achieved. Completed in 1869, the new railroad stretched across 1,774 miles, from Nebraska to California. The new railroad made it possible for people to travel safely across the country in just a few days instead of months!

THE NEW WORLD

In 1492, Christopher Columbus discovered the New World when the *Nina*, *Pinta*, and *Santa Maria* made landfall on the **Caribbean** island of San Salvador. When Columbus arrived on the beach, he kissed the sand and broke into tears. After that, he planted the green and gold flags of Ferdinand and Isabella, the Spanish king and queen. And while Columbus never set foot on what would one day become the United States, he did open the door for European settlers to come to the Americas.

First Voyage: The Christmas Wreck

During his first voyage, Columbus piloted the *Santa Maria*. Unfortunately, he wrecked that ship, running it too close to the coast of **Hispaniola**. He ordered his men to use the timbers from the smashed ship to build the first Spanish fort in the New World. He called that fort La Navidad, since he had wrecked the ship on Christmas Eve.

Second Voyage: Ye Olde Family Road Trip, er…Sea Voyage!

On Columbus' second voyage, he brought seventeen ships containing over 1,200 soldiers and an array of horses, cows, goats, and pigs. In addition to the 1,200 soldiers, historians estimate that as many as 300 female **stowaways**, mostly wives of the troops, came as well. Columbus brought such a large crowd because Ferdinand and Isabella were anxious to populate the newfound lands with Spanish settlers.

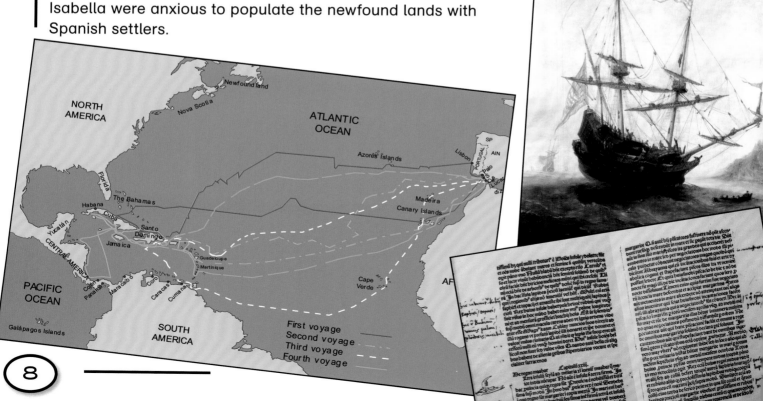

Third Voyage: Columbus In Chains

This trip ended badly, as Columbus was sent home to Spain in chains, having been arrested on Hispaniola by a special agent of King Ferdinand. Spanish colonies in the New World were struggling due to brutal temperatures and disease. As the Spanish death toll mounted, Columbus was blamed. Once back in Spain, Columbus appeared before Ferdinand and Isabella, where he broke down in tears. All was forgiven and he was even allowed to return for a fourth voyage.

Fourth Voyage: Shipwrecked!

On his fourth and final voyage to the New World, Columbus became shipwrecked on Jamaica and was stranded there for a year before finally being rescued. He traded beads and **trinkets** with the natives of the island in exchange for food for himself and his crew.

Where's Columbus?

If you want to visit Columbus' gravesite, you need to go to two different countries to be sure you've definitely seen it. Both Spain and the Dominican Republic have a burial site for the great explorer. Columbus' coffin was dug up and reburied at least five times. In all that movement, it seems that the wrong body may have been dug up, so today it is unclear as to where he is really buried. The Spanish gravesite is a magnificent cathedral in Madrid and the Dominican Republic site is a massive concrete building called the Faro a Colón.

D.Y.K.A.

COLUMBUS' ACCIDENTAL DISCOVERY!

Columbus was actually trying to get to Asia on his first voyage, but accidentally ran into the Bahamas instead. He had no idea the Americas were here, but it's a good thing they were, because his crew did not have nearly enough food to make it to Asia. Columbus and his men would have certainly perished from hunger if the New World had not blocked his path.

TAMING A WILD LAND

Beginning in 1607, English settlers started thirteen colonies along America's Atlantic coastline. These colonies would eventually grow to a population of four million by the time of the Revolutionary War and would make up the first thirteen states of the union. The earliest of these settlements, Jamestown, Virginia, and Plymouth, Massachusetts, experienced the hardest struggles for survival.

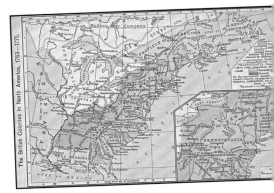

Jamestown Romance?

Pocahontas and John Smith really were friends, although it's unclear if they had a romantic relationship. She was twelve and he was twenty-seven when they met. According to Smith's revised account of their meeting, they met the night Pocahontas saved Smith's life. She threw herself across his body to prevent her father's warriors from killing the Englishman.

Starvation Station

Conditions at the Jamestown colony were brutal. Disease, hunger, dirty drinking water, and constant Indian warfare claimed the lives of 8,800 of the first 10,000 English settlers to arrive in the colony. The worst period for the colony was called the Starving Time, a period in the winter of 1610 in which the colony shrunk from 500 settlers to sixty.

"Please Pass the Eel!"

After sixty-five grueling days at sea, the *Mayflower*'s 102 passengers arrived in modern-day Massachusetts in November 1620. They called their colony Plymouth. Because they arrived too late to build cabins and plant crops, the harsh weather devastated them. By spring, fifty-two of the group were dead. But after that winter, the hardworking Puritans established a thriving colony, largely due to help from the local natives. The friendship that developed between the *Mayflower* survivors and surrounding Indians was very strong.

As a result, they celebrated with a feast in October 1621 that we now call the first Thanksgiving. The menu for that celebration of survival included eel, deer, duck, geese, and turkey, of course!

Settling In

In their first weeks at the Plymouth colony, the settlers saw and heard many signs that Indians were watching them. Needless to say, this was frightening. We can only imagine how stunned they were in March 1621, when a Native American named Samoset walked all the way into the village, stopped, and loudly announced in English, "Welcome, englishmen." As it turns out, a few Indians knew the language from previous contact with traders. This began an important friendship, as the settlers learned survival skills from the natives.

The Indians taught the colonists how to mound up dirt and put corn seeds and herring into it. Once the corn sprouted, they planted squash and beans on the mound as well. The squash covered the ground to retain moisture and prevent weeds, while the beans grew up the corn stalk, making them easy to pick.

REBELLIOUS AMERICANS

Life in the colonies was good for most people. America was a land where many people found the opportunity to start over and build a new life, yet England saw an opportunity to profit from the new colonies. Soon new taxes were added and other laws were made that many colonists saw as intolerable. Worst of all, the colonists were not allowed to elect lawmakers to represent themselves, so they had no way to stop the creation of such laws. How could their mother country do this to them? They were being taxed without representation and the colonists were getting angry!

The Boston Massacre

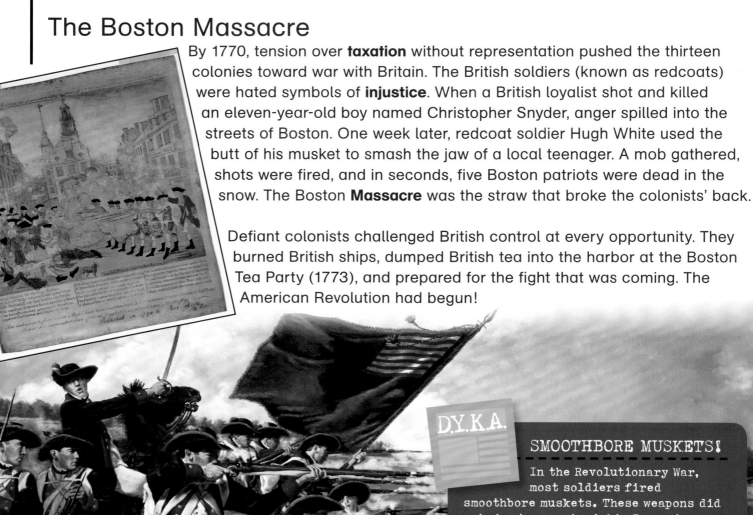

By 1770, tension over **taxation** without representation pushed the thirteen colonies toward war with Britain. The British soldiers (known as redcoats) were hated symbols of **injustice**. When a British loyalist shot and killed an eleven-year-old boy named Christopher Snyder, anger spilled into the streets of Boston. One week later, redcoat soldier Hugh White used the butt of his musket to smash the jaw of a local teenager. A mob gathered, shots were fired, and in seconds, five Boston patriots were dead in the snow. The Boston **Massacre** was the straw that broke the colonists' back.

Defiant colonists challenged British control at every opportunity. They burned British ships, dumped British tea into the harbor at the Boston Tea Party (1773), and prepared for the fight that was coming. The American Revolution had begun!

D.Y.K.A.

SMOOTHBORE MUSKETS!

In the Revolutionary War, most soldiers fired smoothbore muskets. These weapons did not shoot very straight. In coming years, gunmakers began putting a spiral groove (rifling) on the inside of the barrel. Without that rifling, musket balls danced and knuckled as they flew through the air. For example, in the Battle of Concord (April 1775), colonists fired an estimated 75,000 shots, but only hit 250 British soldiers.

"The Regulars Are Coming!"

Though the colonists wrote several letters complaining about their treatment and their rights as English citizens, England continued to punish the colonies for their defiance. Boston, Massachusetts, was particularly filled with rebellious leaders, such as John Adams, his cousin Samuel Adams, John Hancock, James Otis, and the famous Paul Revere.

When England sent troops to Boston to stop these men, Paul Revere rode his horse to warn of the redcoats who were coming to arrest colonists. Two lanterns were hung in the bell tower of Christ's Church as a signal so Revere would know the soldiers were coming by sea. He rode fast from Boston to Lexington, telling everyone, "The regulars are coming! The regulars are coming!" He did not make it to Concord due to being captured by the British, but eventually returned to Lexington, where he would witness one of the first battles for American independence.

Lexington and Concord:
"The Shot Heard 'Round The World"

The British army came to Lexington looking for John Hancock and John Adams, but what they found instead was a group of Minutemen, colonists who were prepared to fight at a minute's notice. One of the Minutemen fired a shot and the battle for freedom began. Though the Minutemen lost that brief battle, the British were met by a larger group of colonists at Concord, where they forced the redcoats to retreat!

The British returned two months later and beat the Americans at Breed's Hill in the Battle of Bunker Hill (June 1775) in Boston. George Washington had just been named the commander in chief of the armies, but the army didn't have enough bullets to fight well. They were so low on ammunition that they were told not to shoot until they saw the "whites of their eyes." Still, the men fought hard and proved they could stand up to the British.

The Declaration of Independence

As more battles were fought, the colonists felt the time was right to tell England they were going to form their own free country, the United States of America. So on July 4, 1776, the leaders of the colonies signed a letter to King George III of England called the Declaration of Independence. England wasn't about to let the colonies go free, so the war continued.

Christmas Surprise

Though the colonists lost many battles, they also won some surprising victories, such as the Battle of Trenton (December 1776). General George Washington knew that enemy soldiers were just across the river from the American forces in Trenton, New Jersey. Knowing the soldiers would be celebrating, Washington ordered the entire army of 2,700 men to cross the icy Delaware River on Christmas night. The next morning, the Americans attacked and captured nearly 1,000 enemy soldiers. Talk about a Christmas surprise! Just days after his big win at Trenton, Washington defeated the British again at nearby Princeton. These two wins in New Jersey gave the Americans a much-needed boost in confidence. And this helped convince many colonists to join in the fight against the British. Even France was impressed and soon gave America help.

Battling Winter

Throughout the war, cold weather was one of the Americans' worst enemies. The coldest winters of the 1700s happened during the Revolutionary War. Many soldiers had very little to keep them warm and very little to eat. During the winter of 1777, over 2,000 men died from the cold and starvation at Valley Forge, Pennsylvania. Many were sick and some even quit the army and went home.

COLONEL ARNOLD

D.Y.K.A.

THE ORIGINAL BENEDICT!

The hero of the Battle of Saratoga (1777) was Benedict Arnold. He bravely led men directly into the most dangerous part of the battlefield. His actions won the battle, but he was severely wounded. Afterwards, his commanding officer took all the credit for the win, leaving Arnold's name out of the battle report to Congress. An infuriated Arnold betrayed his country as a result, and joined the British Army for the rest of the war.

"The World Turn'd Upside Down"

No matter what weather or obstacles they faced, the colonists continued to fight. England was often surprised at how long and hard America would fight. Little by little, the Americans were winning the war. Finally, in October of 1781, the British Army was cut off by the French Navy, and a combined force of French and American soldiers were able to capture the British armies at Yorktown, Virginia. There, British General Charles Cornwallis surrendered his forces. The British soldiers were so shocked at losing, they played a song called, "The World Turn'd Upside Down." Within two years of the surrender, all British soldiers returned to England and America was finally independent.

AWAY WE GROW!

Now that they were free, Americans had to decide what kind of government and laws they wanted. The future of the new country depended on the choices they made. It would become the foundation of freedom and a light to other nations around the world.

The American Experiment

In the summer of 1787, fifty-five representatives from twelve states (Rhode Island was not represented) met in Philadelphia to amend the Articles of Confederation, which were written and ratified months earlier. Instead of changing the Articles of Confederation, they ended up scraping the idea and began work on the US Constitution. A constitution is a set of rules for how the country must operate. Having a constitution is very important in a **democracy**, because it prevents one person or a small group of people from having too much control over the lives of everyone else. The Constitution created the basic government structure that we still use today. It calls for a president who handles foreign affairs and the military, a congress that makes laws, and a court system that makes sure the Constitution is being upheld.

Laying Down the Law: The Whiskey Rebellion

In 1791, the brand-new US federal government placed a tax on Americans who made carriages, molasses, or whiskey. Whiskey is actually made from corn or grain, and it was an important **cash crop** for many farmers. So in 1794, when government tax collectors headed to the backwoods areas of the western Pennsylvania frontier, things got violent. Angry farmers shot at, tarred and feathered, or even killed the government officials. President Washington realized that a government's laws must be enforced or there would be no government. So he pulled out his old Revolutionary War uniform and led soldiers into the area of rebellion. Just the idea of the awesome General Washington leading men into battle had the needed effect. Most of the whiskey rebels fled, twenty were arrested, and the rebellion officially ended. Washington made it clear that if the government says you owe a tax, then you will have to pay it.

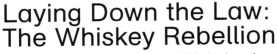

D.Y.K.A.

GEORGE WASHINGTON'S TRIP TO PENNSYLVANIA!

The Whiskey Rebellion is the only time in history that the president of the United States led an army in the field. Many generals would become president, including William Henry Harrison, Zachary Taylor, Ulysses S. Grant, and Dwight Eisenhower, but only the father of our country ever left the White House to take care of military matters himself.

From Sea to Shining Sea: The Louisiana Purchase

The Louisiana Purchase was the greatest land deal ever made. The government paid three cents an acre in 1803 for the territory that is now sixteen states. President Thomas Jefferson had sent a team of negotiators to Paris to offer the French ten million dollars just for the city of New Orleans. But when the French offered to sell over 800,000 square miles for just fifteen million dollars, the men jumped at the offer.

Scouting the New Frontier: Lewis and Clark

Having purchased the Louisiana Territory, Thomas Jefferson sent Meriwether Lewis and William Clark to explore the area. Leaving from St. Louis and traveling all the way to the Pacific Ocean and back, the Lewis and Clark expedition lasted from 1804 to 1806. The thirty-three person group received help from Native American guide Sacagawea, who gave birth to a baby on the trip. Today in St. Louis, the magnificent Gateway Arch stands 630 feet tall, serving as a marker for the beginning of the expedition. The Arch commemorates the city's role as the gateway to the West for Lewis and Clark and thousands of other settlers.

D.Y.K.A.

DUELING PRESIDENTS!

Thomas Jefferson's vice president, Aaron Burr, did something unique while serving as backup to the president; he killed a man in a duel. This exchange of pistol shots took place just outside of New York City in July 1804. Alexander Hamilton and Aaron Burr had repeatedly insulted each other over the years, which led to the duel. Hamilton was shot through the hip and died the next day. Burr was disgraced and never held political office again.

TOUGH TIMES

As the United States grew, England grew jealous and decided to attack the young nation. Yet they would find that Americans were tough people who would defend themselves against any invader.

"Old Hickory" Andrew Jackson

The dominant president of the early 1800s was Andrew Jackson. This tough-skinned hero of the Battle of New Orleans (January 1815) engaged in multiple duels and gun battles as a young man living in Tennessee. The first six American presidents were well-educated men from large eastern cities, but Jackson was a **backwoodsman** of the people. His brand of Jacksonian democracy put the power of the government into the hands of the average American.

D.Y.K.A.

JACKSON'S CLOSE CALL!

Andrew Jackson was the first president to experience an **assassination** attempt. A mentally-ill man named Richard Lawrence approached Jackson in the Capitol building, pulled out two pistols, and pulled the triggers on both. But both guns misfired, meaning the hammer failed to ignite the gunpowder in the pistol. Lawrence was put on trial and judged to be not guilty by reason of insanity, but spent the rest of his life as a prisoner in a mental health hospital.

The Thirty-Day President

William Henry Harrison achieved the sad distinction of being president for the shortest amount of time. Like Andrew Jackson, Harrison was a war hero, known for his victory at the Battle of Tippecanoe (November 1811). He was sworn in on March 4, 1841, and caught a bad cold three weeks later. The cold turned to pneumonia and he died in the White House on April 4. He was president for only thirty days.

British Bullies: The War of 1812

The United States fought a second war with Great Britain from 1812 to 1815. It was called The War of 1812 and it ended in a **cease-fire**. Interestingly, the "Star-Spangled Banner" was written during the war. As Francis Scott Key watched "the rockets' red glare" while British bombs burst in the air over Baltimore's Fort McHenry, he wrote the words to the song on an envelope.

Burning Down the House

The War of 1812 also resulted in the destruction of some part of Washington, DC. It was our brand new capital; James Madison was only the third president to live there when the British burned down most of the buildings in the city, including the White House, Capitol, and Library of Congress. First Lady Dolley Madison had just sat down to dinner when she was warned the British were coming. She quickly sliced a priceless oil portrait of George Washington from its frame and fled the city. The fire was put out by a huge rainstorm.

D.Y.K.A.

O.K.!

The expression "O.K." started with president Martin Van Buren, who served from 1837-1841. Van Buren was from Kinderhook, New York, and was often referred to as "Old Kinderhook," or "O.K." for short. This expression caught on to mean something is all right. In the presidential election of 1840, it became a big part of the campaign to get Van Buren re-elected. He did not win that election, but at least his phrase lives on.

A Growing Argument

During the 1840s and 1850s, the issue of slavery divided Americans. Politicians worked feverishly to create solutions to the situation, but in the end all attempts at compromise failed. Only the bloodiest war in American history could resolve the issues of this period.

SOUTHERN CHIVALRY — ARGUMENT versus CLUB'S.

Cane Of Wrath

On May 22, 1856, South Carolina Congressman Preston Brooks approached the desk of Massachusetts Senator Charles Sumner. Brooks announced, "You have slandered my state… and it is my duty to punish you." With that, he began to savagely beat Sumner with a cane, hitting him over and over, until the cane broke into pieces. Brooks walked away, leaving Sumner unconscious and bloodied. Two days earlier, Sumner had given a speech in which he criticized slavery and South Carolina. Sumner survived, but could not return to work for three years.

D.Y.K.A.

POLITICIANS: ARMED & DANGEROUS!

Tensions were so high in the days before the Civil War that congressmen in Washington, DC, feared to enter the Capitol building unarmed. A fistfight broke out on the floor of the senate in 1858 involving many members. It started when a southern senator attempted to strangle a senator from Pennsylvania. Said one senator in 1859, "Every man in both houses is armed with a revolver, some with two, and a bowie knife."

The Slave Trade

Of the nine million Americans who lived in the southern United States in 1860, four million were enslaved African-American laborers. In some areas with large plantations in the Deep South, slaves outnumbered free people ten to one.

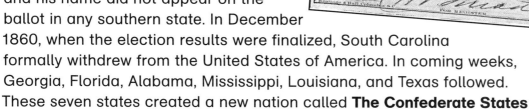

A New Nation?

Abraham Lincoln won the presidential election of 1860. However, he only took thirty-nine percent of the popular vote, and his name did not appear on the ballot in any southern state. In December 1860, when the election results were finalized, South Carolina formally withdrew from the United States of America. In coming weeks, Georgia, Florida, Alabama, Mississippi, Louisiana, and Texas followed. These seven states created a new nation called **The Confederate States of America**. They elected Jefferson Davis as president and wrote a constitution that allowed for slavery. After the war began, four more states, North Carolina, Virginia, Tennessee, and Arkansas, joined the CSA.

Fighting the Numbers

The eleven Confederate States of America found themselves at a disadvantage in nearly every statistical category as they moved toward war. Of the ten largest cities in America, only one, New Orleans, was in the South. Ninety percent of the nation's factories were in the North as well. There were twice as many horses and cows in the North and nearly all the nation's coal and iron came from there. Over twenty million people lived in the North, while only nine million lived in the South.

A House Divided

In the last years before the Civil War, many episodes highlighted how the nation was divided over slavery. In the mid-1850s, over fifty people died fighting over slave rights in the states of Kansas and Missouri. In 1857, the Supreme Court infuriated northerners by ruling in the Dred Scott decision that slaves could not be citizens of the United States. And in 1859, John Brown attempted to liberate the slaves of Virginia in his daring raid on Harper's Ferry. He hoped to use weapons from the federal arsenal there to arm slaves. However, the attempt failed and twenty-five people died in the attack or in the hangings that followed.

A Nation at War with Itself

Even after southern states **seceded** to form their own country, Abraham Lincoln promised he would not try to force them to outlaw slavery. His goal was to keep the United States together, and he would not accept their secession. Though he hoped to resolve the matter peacefully, the southern states took over several military forts including Fort Sumter, South Carolina (April 1861), and the nation fell into Civil War.

Whose Side Are You On?

The war divided more than a country; it divided families. Many people had family members who lived in both the North and the South. Some even joined opposite armies. Most of them didn't have uniforms in the early battles, so telling a northern or Union soldier apart from a southern or Confederate soldier was confusing to say the least.

At the Battle of Bull Run (July 1861), men arrived for battle wearing every color of the rainbow. This included purples, reds, yellows, stripes, Scottish plaids, and even firefighter's outfits from their hometowns. Brutal confusion pushed both armies to outfit men uniformly. The Union wore blue and the Confederates wore gray or **butternut**.

The Soldiers' Life

As awful as war was, it was also boring. On average, men saw battle seven days a year. So there was a lot of free time. Playing baseball was one way men passed the time. Once in Texas, a Union soldier playing baseball wandered too near Confederate lines in center field and was shot. The **Rebel** troops kept the ball. For southern soldiers, hunger made the boredom worse. They often found worms or maggots in their food. Shortages were so severe for the Confederates that occasionally they were fed mule meat. Interestingly, when soldiers from the two sides encountered each other in non-battle situations, they often stopped to visit. They would talk at water holes, swim together, and trade papers, coffee, and information.

D.Y.K.A.

THE GLAMOROUS WAR!

At the time of the Civil War, fighting for your country in a battle was considered a great honor. Volunteers proudly paraded through town in their newly formed military units as they marched off to war. Yet many of them were poorly trained, and the excitement of war quickly changed when they saw their friends and fellow soldiers die. War was anything but glamorous.

Cotton Power

As a major grower of cotton for the world, the South felt the world needed their cotton so much that they would be able to get France or England to help them fight—something called **cotton diplomacy**. However, the world soon turned to other cotton growers, such as India or Egypt, and the South never got the help they needed.

The Northern Edge

The North had factories to make ammunition and supplies. They had better transportation, communication, and manpower. Their railroads allowed them to quickly move troops and supplies from place to place. Their navy controlled the rivers and seaports, cutting off the South from needed supplies. The invention of the telegraph allowed instructions to be relayed over vast distances in seconds, which gave the North the information they needed to plan and move the armies. Add to that the fact that the North had over twenty million inhabitants to the South's nine million, four million of which were slaves.

Following the Leader

Despite the lack of numbers, the South more than made up for their disadvantage with superior leadership. The Union Army was led by men who either made poor battlefield decisions or hesitated long enough for the enemy to escape capture. It particularly frustrated President Lincoln who wanted to save lives and end the war as soon as possible.

The Confederate Army was lead by General Robert E. Lee, a graduate of the US Military Academy at West Point and a brilliant battle planner. Lincoln actually offered Lee command of the Union Army, but he felt he had to defend his home state of Virginia and resigned from the army. He joined a host of fellow West Point graduates who served under him as generals. Lee was able to consistently win battles even when he was outnumbered, such as Chancellorsville (May 1863), where he took 56,000 men and beat a Union Army of 135,000.

Body Count

Victories and losses came at a great cost though. Thousands died in each battle. The Battle of Gettysburg (July 1863) was the largest and most destructive of the war. When it was over, one street in the town had thirty dead horses. A nearby tree had 250 musket balls and 27,000 muskets were found on the battlefield (24,000 were still loaded)! Worst of all, over 7,000 men lay dead after the three days of terrible fighting.

A Short Address

Four months after the Battle of Gettysburg, President Lincoln gave his famous Gettysburg Address on the battlefield. The speech was 272 words and lasted two minutes and fifteen seconds. This oration is remembered as the greatest ever given in America. Remarkably, a dignitary from Massachusetts spoke before Lincoln that day, and his speech lasted two hours!

Breaking the South

Finally, Lincoln found a leader to end the war in General Ulysses S. Grant. Once he took over as commander, the tide of the war began to shift. As the battles became more desperate, the brave Confederate generals led their soldiers in a fight against the odds. In the end, their courageous actions cost them their lives and left their men without the leadership they needed to win.

In fact, at the Battle of Franklin (November 1864) six Confederate generals fell, six were wounded and one was captured, while nearly 2,000 soldiers died and 4,000 were injured in a single afternoon. This blow further crippled the already weak Confederate Army. In April of 1865, Lee was forced to surrender at Appomattox Court House, Virginia.

Losing Lincoln

On April 14, 1865, President Lincoln sat watching a play in Ford's Theater in Washington, DC. John Wilkes Booth slipped behind him, extended his single shot derringer pistol, and pulled the trigger. The half-inch-wide bullet entered the president's head behind his left ear, traveled diagonally across his brain, and lodged behind his right eye. President Lincoln's head slumped to his chest; he would never regain consciousness. He was placed on a wooden door and carried across the street to a boarding house, where he died at 7:22 a.m.

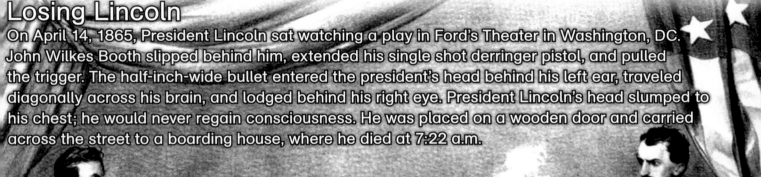

Freeing the Slaves, Constitutionally Speaking

Part of Lincoln's legacy was the Emancipation Proclamation issued in 1863 during the Civil War. It freed the slaves in some states, but not others. To extend that freedom to all slaves in all states, a constitutional amendment was needed. A constitutional amendment is an addition to the original Constitution. It must be approved or ratified by a vote of a majority of states (seventy-four percent). In 1865, just a year after Lincoln's death, the Thirteenth Amendment was approved and slavery was officially outlawed in the United States. Lincoln's dream was law!

RECONSTRUCTING AMERICA

After the Civil War, the nation needed healing, so America got busy. They headed for the wide-open spaces of the Wild West. Some built railroads, while others herded cattle or grew crops in the fertile soil of the prairies. Americans were also hard at work creating new inventions, and soon they were soaring beyond their wildest dreams.

Spanning the Continent

In the 1840s, Americans began to dream of a railroad that could bridge the nation's 2,000-mile gap between its East and West coasts. Immense mountains, brutal deserts, and countless rivers made the task seem nearly impossible. Yet the US government was convinced it could be done, and in 1862 they contracted two companies to start a transcontinental railroad with one end starting in Missouri and the other end starting in California. The two railroads connected just north of the Great Salt Lake on May 10, 1869, at Promontory Point, Utah. Coming just four years after the Civil War, the transcontinental railroad gave the nation a much-needed and well-earned burst of pride and unity.

The Wild West

Though the **Gold Rush** of 1849 brought many settlers out West seeking their fortune, the Homestead Act of 1862 gave 160 acres of land to anyone willing to live on it for five years. It lured many new farmers to the West, but it was the completion of several railroads that attracted cattle ranchers. The ranchers or cowboys would herd their cattle on long cattle drives across huge territories to the railroads where they could ship cattle that cost four dollars each to the cattle markets in the eastern United States. There they could sell them for forty dollars each!

Railroad cattle depots such as Abilene and Dodge City, Kansas, were huge gathering places for cowboys at the end of the trail. But when the cowboys went looking for trouble, frontier sheriffs, such as the famous Wyatt Earp, enforced the laws. Yet gunslinging cowboys soon faded into history. As the railroads expanded into new areas, long cattle drives were no longer necessary. The invention of barbed wire in 1873 also allowed landowners to cut off traditional cattle trails. Before long, the open range was closed and the Wild West became civilized.

The Edison Effect

No one person was responsible for America's rise to greatness after the Civil War, but Thomas Edison certainly led the way. Edison patented over 1,000 of his inventions, including the record player, the light bulb, and the movie camera. Edison also developed methods for generating and moving electric current through cities. His electric generators and light bulbs literally lit New York City for the first time in 1882. Edison's movie camera led to the opening of America's first nickelodeon movie theater in Pittsburgh in 1905, where you could watch short films for—you guessed it—a nickel!

Jazzing It Up!

In the late 1800s, the record player created a huge demand for new music. Scott Joplin's Ragtime music filled this need. His famous "Maple Leaf Rag" came out in 1899, featuring a stunning syncopated rhythm. Next came jazz music, which originated in New Orleans, Louisiana, as early as 1913. African-American musicians developed this exciting form of music and soon Americans everywhere were dancing. Flapper dresses were the rage and party-goers stayed up late doing dances with names like the Grizzly Bear, the Turkey Trot, and the Bunny Hug.

Soaring!

Though many inventors worked to develop flying machines, Orville and Wilbur Wright were the first humans to truly fly. Applying their knowledge as bicycle mechanics, these two brothers flew their homemade airplane 120 feet over the sand dunes of Kitty Hawk, North Carolina, on December 17, 1903. They continued to improve their airplane, and in 1909, they did a demonstration in New York City, with Wilbur soaring around the Statue of Liberty. Suddenly, America had wings!

THE WAR TO END ALL WARS: WORLD WAR I

In August of 1914, a new kind of war ravaged the European continent. Great powers such as Russia, France, Italy, and Britain fought against Germany and Austria-Hungary in a clash that eventually involved most of Europe and the Middle East. Modern technology brought the flamethrower, tanks, poisonous gas, and the machine gun together onto the battlefield for the first time. This created a nightmare in which thousands died every day until the war ended in 1918. World War I was known as the Great War until an even larger war (World War II) broke out just twenty-one years later.

Ship of Death: *Lusitania*

On May 1, 1915, the British passenger ship *Lusitania* departed New York City carrying nearly 2,000 people. The massive vessel was the fastest and most luxurious ship in the world. However, besides carrying civilian passengers, it also carried six million rifle bullets and 500,000 pounds of **artillery** shells. These were for use by the British army in World War I. Germany was aware of the cargo and posted a warning in New York newspapers that they might sink the ship. The warning was not taken seriously and the ship, bound for London, nearly made it across the Atlantic. But when a German **U-Boat** spotted the ship just thirty miles south of Ireland, it fired a **torpedo**. The *Lusitania* exploded and sunk in just eighteen minutes. Over a thousand people died, including 128 Americans. America would never forget and entered into WWI on the side of France and Britain two years later.

D.Y.K.A.

A COUNTRY HERO!

During World War I, Alvin C. York became America's greatest war hero when he personally captured 132 German soldiers and killed twenty-eight more. York was an expert marksman who developed his skills by shooting turkeys as a boy in Tennessee. He was so skilled that he only fired his pistol and rifle twenty-eight times on the day he became famous. After the war, he was thrown a **ticker-tape parade** in New York City. He then went home where the governor of Tennessee presided as Alvin married his hometown sweetheart, Gracie, and the citizens of the state all chipped in to buy him a farm.

Outbreak! The Flu of 1918

In February 1918, an influenza virus that started in Kansas spread through US Army troops as they went overseas for World War I. The virus ravaged Europe, Africa, and Asia, and then returned to the United States in September of that same year. It killed 650,000 Americans in six months. This tragedy killed nearly the same number of Americans as the Civil War, but did so in just one-eighth of the time. Hysteria swept the nation, as Americans feared to speak to neighbors or leave their houses. Schools closed, people wore gauze masks, and cities passed laws against spitting and handshaking. When the virus finally disappeared in 1919, it left between twenty and fifty million dead worldwide, a tragedy comparable to World War II.

THE BIG ONE:
WORLD WAR II IN EUROPE

The Great Depression affected more than just America. Countries around the world were experiencing similar hard times. They lost faith in their governments and turned to their military to help make things right. Germany elected a new leader, Adolf Hitler. Though Germany was forbidden to have a large military after World War I, Hitler built a huge army and air force. Then he began invading neighboring countries.

Blitzkrieg: The Lightning War

World War II began on September 1, 1939, in Europe when Adolf Hitler's German Army invaded Poland. He told his troops to "have no pity" and carry out the campaign with "the greatest brutality and without mercy." Hitler's fast-moving Panzer tanks dominated the Polish cavalry while his Stuka dive bombers destroyed the entire Polish air force in forty-eight hours. Britain and France declared war on Germany as soon as the invasion began, but could do nothing to rescue the Poles, who surrendered after twenty-eight days. During the six year German occupation, sixteen percent of the Polish population died. This included 3.5 million Jews, which was nearly every Jewish person living in the country.

D.Y.K.A.

THE RUBBER TANK DECEPTION!

Hundreds of inflatable rubber tanks were placed in Dover, England, prior to D-Day to convince the Germans the invasion would come from there. It worked! Hitler placed his best Panzer units directly across the English Channel from Dover. When the actual invasion landed 100 miles away, those Panzers missed the battle.

The Building Battle

After defeating Poland, Germany went on to conquer or make alliances with nearly all of Europe and northern Africa. Next Hitler launched the largest land invasion in history, using three million troops to invade the Soviet Union in 1941. He also declared war on the United States, though German forces never reached American shores. Hitler's grand plans overextended German forces. They could not hold and defend a territory that stretched over 2,000 miles at its peak in 1942. The US Army invaded northern Africa to begin a slow rollback of the Germans, while Russia held its own in Eastern Europe In 1942.

Ship of Death: *Lusitania*

On May 1, 1915, the British passenger ship *Lusitania* departed New York City carrying nearly 2,000 people. The massive vessel was the fastest and most luxurious ship in the world. However, besides carrying civilian passengers, it also carried six million rifle bullets and 500,000 pounds of **artillery** shells. These were for use by the British army in World War I. Germany was aware of the cargo and posted a warning in New York newspapers that they might sink the ship. The warning was not taken seriously and the ship, bound for London, nearly made it across the Atlantic. But when a German **U-Boat** spotted the ship just thirty miles south of Ireland, it fired a **torpedo**. The *Lusitania* exploded and sunk in just eighteen minutes. Over a thousand people died, including 128 Americans. America would never forget and entered into WWI on the side of France and Britain two years later.

D.Y.K.A.

A COUNTRY HERO!

During World War I, Alvin C. York became America's greatest war hero when he personally captured 132 German soldiers and killed twenty-eight more. York was an expert marksman who developed his skills by shooting turkeys as a boy in Tennessee. He was so skilled that he only fired his pistol and rifle twenty-eight times on the day he became famous. After the war, he was thrown a **ticker-tape parade** in New York City. He then went home where the governor of Tennessee presided as Alvin married his hometown sweetheart, Gracie, and the citizens of the state all chipped in to buy him a farm.

Outbreak! The Flu of 1918

In February 1918, an influenza virus that started in Kansas spread through US Army troops as they went overseas for World War I. The virus ravaged Europe, Africa, and Asia, and then returned to the United States in September of that same year. It killed 650,000 Americans in six months. This tragedy killed nearly the same number of Americans as the Civil War, but did so in just one-eighth of the time. Hysteria swept the nation, as Americans feared to speak to neighbors or leave their houses. Schools closed, people wore gauze masks, and cities passed laws against spitting and handshaking. When the virus finally disappeared in 1919, it left between twenty and fifty million dead worldwide, a tragedy comparable to World War II.

BOOM TO BUST

After World War I, Americans experienced a wave of **prosperity** as they had money to spend and time to spend it. For example, in 1920, Americans spent ten million dollars on radios, but in 1929 they spent 411 million dollars. In particular, everyone wanted an automobile. Cars were so popular that the Ford Motor Company alone employed 5,000 janitors and had twenty-seven miles of conveyor belts at its Detroit facility. No wonder it was called the **roaring twenties**!

Race to Greatness

The twenties was also a decade of excitement. Charles Lindbergh flew across the Atlantic, jazz music brought record numbers onto the dance floor, and a skyscraper race changed the face of New York City. America's tallest building, the amazingly beautiful Chrysler building, was completed in 1929 in New York. But it was only tallest for a few months. In 1930, the Empire State Building became the tallest building in New York, as well as in the world, measuring 1,250 feet high.

The Crash

The Great **Depression** began in October 1929, when the US **stock market** crashed, meaning that thirty billion dollars in stocks and bonds disappeared in five days. That dollar figure was ten times greater than the entire federal government budget for the year, so the loss was truly colossal. As a result, one third of Americans lost their jobs. Most Americans who had money saved in banks lost it forever, and sixty percent of Midwest farmers lost their farms. The value of the US stock market did not return to its 1929 level until 1954.

A New Hope

In 1932, Franklin Delano Roosevelt was elected president, and his efforts to fight the Great Depression were called the New Deal. He stimulated the economy by creating jobs and building projects. Thousands of parks and bridges were built, four billion trees were planted, and millions of men were put to work. The New Deal pumped needed money into the economy, but only the arrival of World War II ended the twelve-year-long Great Depression.

FDR: Leading America Through the Storms

Franklin Delano Roosevelt was the only US president elected more than twice; he was actually elected four times in 1932, '36, '40, and '44. Americans kept him in office because his strong leadership seemed essential during the back-to-back crises of the Great Depression and World War II.

D.Y.K.A.

THE PRESIDENT'S SECRET!

FDR was the only president who could not walk. Polio struck him eleven years before his election, paralyzing him from the waist down. He kept this hidden from the American public by being careful to not be photographed in his wheelchair.

31

THE BIG ONE:
WORLD WAR II IN EUROPE

The Great Depression affected more than just America. Countries around the world were experiencing similar hard times. They lost faith in their governments and turned to their military to help make things right. Germany elected a new leader, Adolf Hitler. Though Germany was forbidden to have a large military after World War I, Hitler built a huge army and air force. Then he began invading neighboring countries.

Blitzkrieg: The Lightning War

World War II began on September 1, 1939, in Europe when Adolf Hitler's German Army invaded Poland. He told his troops to "have no pity" and carry out the campaign with "the greatest brutality and without mercy." Hitler's fast-moving Panzer tanks dominated the Polish cavalry while his Stuka dive bombers destroyed the entire Polish air force in forty-eight hours. Britain and France declared war on Germany as soon as the invasion began, but could do nothing to rescue the Poles, who surrendered after twenty-eight days. During the six year German occupation, sixteen percent of the Polish population died. This included 3.5 million Jews, which was nearly every Jewish person living in the country.

D.Y.K.A.

THE RUBBER TANK DECEPTION!

Hundreds of inflatable rubber tanks were placed in Dover, England, prior to D-Day to convince the Germans the invasion would come from there. It worked! Hitler placed his best Panzer units directly across the English Channel from Dover. When the actual invasion landed 100 miles away, those Panzers missed the battle.

The Building Battle

After defeating Poland, Germany went on to conquer or make alliances with nearly all of Europe and northern Africa. Next Hitler launched the largest land invasion in history, using three million troops to invade the Soviet Union in 1941. He also declared war on the United States, though German forces never reached American shores. Hitler's grand plans overextended German forces. They could not hold and defend a territory that stretched over 2,000 miles at its peak in 1942. The US Army invaded northern Africa to begin a slow rollback of the Germans, while Russia held its own in Eastern Europe In 1942.

D-Day: America Strikes Back!

On June 6, 1944, the United States and its allies launched the largest **amphibious** invasion in world history. Six thousand boats participated in landing 138,000 men on German-held France's Normandy beaches that day. The fifty-mile-wide beach was divided into sections with code names Utah, Omaha, Gold, Juno, and Sword. The heaviest fighting was at Omaha, because extra German troops happened to be there for training exercises. By the end of the day, the Allies held the beaches, and over the next month, one million troops used this as their doorway to Nazi-occupied Europe.

D.Y.K.A.

BOATS THAT PACK A PUNCH!

US beach landing crafts were called Higgins boats, and each carried a thirty-two-man landing team: seven men with rifles, four men with Browning automatic rifles or machine guns, two men armed with flamethrowers, four men using bazookas (anti-tank weapons), four men with mortars (tubes that launched explosive shells), five demolition men to blow up bunkers or obstacles, two medics to help the wounded, and four wire cutters to slice through any barbed wire obstacles.

The War Machine

A primary reason for US victory in WWI was its ability to make war materials quickly. One example was the Liberty Ship. In 1940, Britain asked the United States to make sixty large cargo ships. There was a shortage due to German submarine attacks. It took 355 days to make the first Liberty Ship, but then the process sped up forty-five days per ship. Contests were held among ship builders and eventually a ship was created in four days. Instead of making sixty of these 420-foot-long ships, the United States manufactured 2,700. The United States out-produced everyone else in the war. When WWII began, the United States had seven **aircraft carriers**. By war's end, it had 109. Three hundred thousand airplanes, 70,000 tanks, and forty-one billion bullets were made during the war.

THE WAR IN THE PACIFIC

Like Germany, Japan had also endured some hard times and turned to their military to make them great. They began by launching a war against China. Then they became friends with Germany and their other ally, Italy. Together they formed the Axis Powers in 1940, vowing to help each other win their battles. And though America tried to stay out of World War II, Japan was determined to push them into the conflict.

"A Day That Will Live In Infamy"

WWII began for the United States on December 7, 1941, when 353 Japanese aircrafts attacked the US Pacific fleet at Pearl Harbor, Hawaii. Caught by surprise, seven of the eight battleships present were sunk or damaged. One battleship, the USS *Oklahoma*, rolled completely upside down after seven torpedoes struck its port side. The worst losses came on the USS *Arizona*, which had a Japanese bomb explode in its ammunition storage room. The massive detonation caused the ship to leap fifteen feet in the water and break in half. The fireball from the explosion rose 500 feet in the air, and over 1,000 men perished.

D.Y.K.A.

THE FLYING SUPERFORTRESS!

The massive B-29 was the largest and most powerful bomber in WWII, capable of dropping 20,000 pounds of bombs, more than twice the capacity of any other bomber. It could fly 4,200 miles on the 7,000 gallons of gas contained in its twenty-two fuel tanks. As a result, the United States could strike Japan from far away air bases in the central Pacific.

Island Hopping

In the hours and days after Pearl Harbor, Japan struck targets around the Pacific. They conquered twenty million square miles of territory, the largest section of the globe ever controlled by one nation. It would be the job of the United States to take this land back. This effort was called island hopping, as American soldiers invaded island after island, fighting the Japanese on beaches and in jungles for four long years. One brutal example of this fighting was Iwo Jima. On this tiny island, 7,000 US Marines died and more **Medals of Honor** (twenty-seven) were awarded than in any other battle.

The Atomic Age

The world entered the nuclear age when the first ever **atomic bomb** was detonated in the New Mexico desert in July 1945. The explosion caused sand to turn to green glass for 400 feet around the blast site. The light flash could be seen 180 miles away, and a mushroom cloud rose 40,000 feet into the air. As a result, the Japanese were given a warning called the Potsdam Ultimatum, telling them to surrender or face utter destruction. The warning was ignored, and the first atomic bomb was dropped on Japan two weeks later.

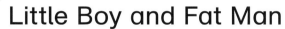

Little Boy and Fat Man

The first atomic bomb (Little Boy) weighed 9,000 pounds, but the key ingredient was 140 pounds of highly radioactive bomb grade uranium 235. Surrounded by thousands of pounds of TNT, the bomb detonated as planned, 1,903 feet over the city of Hiroshima, Japan, on August 6, 1945. A flash of light four times brighter than the sun vaporized all life for a quarter mile around the explosion. A mushroom cloud of boiling red and yellow dust measuring 5,600°F scorched the area, and a pressure wave in the form of a 980 mph wind knocked down trees and buildings throughout the city. Still, Japan refused to surrender. Three days later, a second atomic bomb (Fat Man) was dropped on Nagasaki, Japan. Finally, the Japanese surrendered and the war came to an end.

POST-WAR PROSPERITY

When World War II ended in 1945, fifteen million US soldiers came home ready to spend money and get married. A **baby boom** took place, and subdivisions were invented as Americans bought houses in record numbers. Lawnmower sales increased by 400 percent in the decade, and the number of Little Leagues rose by 800 percent. The first subdivision, Levittown, was built in 1947 in New York and consisted of 17,207 houses.

Captivated by a Box

In 1948, the big three networks, CBS, ABC, and NBC, all began to broadcast television programs over the airwaves. By 1950, it was clear that TV was here to stay. Americans were fascinated by television, and the first family on the street to get one was guaranteed to get lots of visitors. Americans loved TV so much, they did not want to stop watching for dinner. Thus, in 1954, the Swanson Company invented TV dinners, frozen food that could be heated up and then easily eaten on a tray while watching the evening shows.

"Hey Lucy!"

The first really big TV show in America was *I Love Lucy*, which debuted on October 15, 1951. Within four months, it was the number one show on television and dominated the ratings for the rest of the decade. The show aired on Monday nights and often two-thirds of the nation's TVs were tuned in. Some stores even closed on Monday nights since everyone was home watching Lucy.

D.Y.K.A.

THE BABY BOOM!

The most popular episode ever of *I Love Lucy* aired on January 19, 1953, when Lucille Ball, who was actually pregnant, gave birth on the show. That night, seventy-one percent of the nation's TVs tuned in, while only sixty-seven percent watched President Eisenhower's inauguration the next day.

THE RISE OF THE GOLDEN ARCHES!

In the 1950s, Richard and Maurice McDonald changed the way Americans eat. They spent the 1940s perfecting their menu at their first restaurant in San Bernardino, California. Next, they began to open McDonald's restaurants around the nation, starting in 1955 with the help of franchiser Ray Kroc. They established their standard burger to be 1.6 ounces of beef, with a tablespoon of ketchup, a teaspoon of mustard, two pickles, and one-quarter ounce of diced onion. That burger remains the same today. By 1960, there were 228 McDonald's restaurants in America, and now there are over 31,000 locations worldwide in 119 countries.

We Like Ike

For eight years during the 1950s, the American president was the highly popular Dwight D. Eisenhower. Known as "Ike," he became famous for successfully leading the 1944 D-Day invasion of Europe. When World War II ended, both political parties hoped he would accept their offer to be their candidate. He ran in 1952 as a Republican, giving the White House back to that party for the first time since 1933. Ike loved golf and played nearly every day as president; he even had a putting green installed in the backyard of the White House.

THE COLD WAR

As soon as the Germans and Japanese were defeated to end WWII, the United States inherited a new opponent, the Soviet Union. At the end of WWII, twenty-three Asian and East European nations made up the Soviet Union. Russia, a nation so large it contains eleven time zones, was the dominant member. The Soviets were committed to expanding their **communist** philosophy across the globe. The Cold War was the forty-five-year effort by the United States to stop that global expansion.

Stealing Nuclear Thunder

In 1949, the four-year period in which the United States was the only nation with an atomic bomb ended as the Soviets tested their first bomb. US scientists suspected the technology had been stolen. They were proved correct when the FBI arrested Julius and Ethel Rosenberg, and charged them with stealing atomic secrets. They had obtained the secrets from other spies at Los Alamos, a top nuclear research facility. The Rosenbergs were executed in New York State's electric chair in 1953. Years later, it was revealed that Ethel was not involved in the spy ring.

One War, Two Koreas

When Soviet-backed North Korean troops invaded South Korea in June 1950, President Harry S. Truman immediately sent in the US Army to prevent the fall of the nation. This war was like a track meet as troops ran up and down the peninsula. The South Korean capital, Seoul, actually changed hands four times. The United States was winning the war until November of 1950, when 300,000 communist Chinese troops blew across the North Korean border. They drove the US Army backwards over 500 miles in the longest retreat in US history. When US troops finally stabilized a military front along the 38th Parallel, a line on a map that cuts across the waist of the peninsula, Truman was ready to play for a tie. All armies held at that point for two years, until a cease-fire was proclaimed in July 1953. Although shooting has stopped, a state of war still exists today between North and South Korea.

The Stratofortress

In 1952, the United States developed the **hydrogen bomb**, a nuclear weapon hundreds of times more powerful than the original atomic bomb. The Soviets obtained the H-bomb two years later. Now the superpowers needed massive jet bombers capable of delivering these bombs halfway around the globe. In 1952, the United States introduced the B-52 Stratofortress, and it carried 66,000 pounds of bombs, could fly 8,500 miles, and was powered by eight jet engines. The Soviets developed a similar jet called the Bison, and these two planes drastically increased the level of danger during the Cold War.

A Dangerous Race

In 1957, the Soviet Union launched the world's first Intercontinental Ballistic Missile (ICBM). This was a rocket capable of carrying a hydrogen bomb as its payload. Two months later, the Soviets launched *Sputnik*, a rocket that placed the world's first **satellite** into orbit around the Earth. As this communist technology regularly passed over the United States, Americans were alarmed and angered. Things only got worse the following month when *Sputnik II* was launched, carrying a dog named Loika. Americans referred to her as Curly. Determined not to lose the space race, the United States rushed its own rocket, *Vanguard*, to the launch pad in December 1957. As the world watched on live TV, the massive but unmanned rocket rose a few feet in the air before crumpling into a gigantic fireball.

CIVIL RIGHTS: THE QUEST FOR EQUALITY

Communism wasn't the only looming threat for America. Race relations in America had always been a problem and though the African-American slaves had been set free in the 1800s, things were never very equal. Blacks were **segregated** from whites. In many places, they were not allowed to go to the same schools as white people or even use the same restrooms or drinking fountains in public. Finally, years of frustration boiled over into action and the quest for civil rights began.

Standing Her Ground

Forty-three-year-old African-American Rosa Parks sparked the **Civil Rights Movement** in 1955. She was arrested in Montgomery, Alabama, for refusing to give up her bus seat for a white man. Reacting to this injustice, Rev. Dr. Martin Luther King Jr. led black citizens of the city in a year long boycott of all city buses. Montgomery typically collected 35,000 bus fares a day, but during the boycott almost no one at all rode the buses. Finally, in December 1956, the city changed its laws, allowing any citizen to sit anywhere they wanted on a bus.

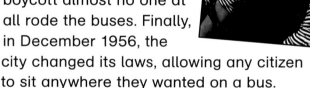

The Little Rock Nine

In 1957, the city of Little Rock, Arkansas, decided to become the first southern city to integrate white and black children in the same school. They invited nine African-American students to enroll at the 2,000-student all-white Little Rock Central High School. However, Governor Orval Faubus did not want **integration** to occur. He placed 270 Arkansas National Guardsmen around the high school to keep out the nine black students. In response, President Dwight Eisenhower sent in US Army troops to escort the students to school each day. Even so, the Little Rock Nine experienced all types of abuse, including being stabbed, beaten, and having flaming paper wads thrown at them.

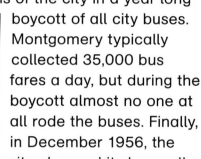

"I Have a Dream"

One of the largest gatherings in US history took place on August 28, 1963, when 250,000 people came to Washington, DC. They were there to protest for civil rights for African-Americans. Famous musicians Joan Baez and Bob Dylan both performed, but the crowd was there to hear the stirring words of Dr. King. His speech was a **watershed moment** in US history: "I have a dream that my four children will one day live in a nation where they will not be judged by the color of their skin, but the content of their character..."

Breaking the Color Barrier

In September 1962, James Meredith attempted to become the first African-American to enroll at the University of Mississippi. To prevent this, Governor Ross Barnett physically stopped him from registering twice. Robert F. Kennedy, the US Attorney General, spoke with Governor Barnett and got him to agree to allow Meredith to register. Yet, when Meredith did register, white students protested and caused a riot. Kennedy sent in 500 US Marshals, and his older brother, President John F. Kennedy, sent in military police as well as the Mississippi National Guard to try to restore order. Unfortunately, two people were killed in the violence, and nearly 200 marshals and soldiers were injured. Once peace was restored, the marshals escorted Meredith to his classes every day until he graduated the next summer with a degree in political science.

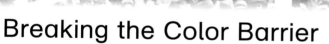

FEATS AND FAILURES

The American story has always been a tale of triumph and tragedy. As the USA inched closer to its 200th birthday, the headlines were filled with amazing feats as well as a few failures. Still, the spirit of '76 lives on in this great nation called the United States of America.

Man on the Moon

In 1961, President Kennedy challenged the nation to do what it took to land a man on the moon, and in response the Apollo space missions began. The program's first launch attempt ended in tragedy. During a training session on the launch pad, the cabin of *Apollo 1* caught fire and the three astronauts trapped inside all died. Their names were Gus Grissom, Ed White, and Roger Chaffee. However, two years later, on July 20, 1969, President Kennedy's dream was fulfilled when the *Apollo 11* lunar module landed on the moon. After stepping from the craft and onto the moon's surface, astronaut Neil Armstrong famously said, "That's one small step for man, one giant leap for mankind."

D.Y.K.A.

THE LUNAR LEGACY!

Apollo 11 was not the United States' only lunar landing. Between 1969 and 1972, the Apollo program landed men on the moon six times. During those trips, twelve different NASA astronauts walked on the moon's surface. On each trip, moon dust and rocks were collected for study here on Earth. Besides the six Apollo Moon landings, no other humans have been to the moon.

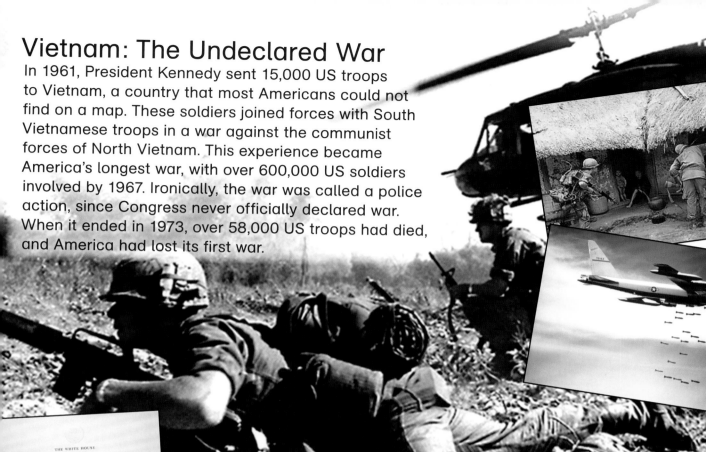

Vietnam: The Undeclared War

In 1961, President Kennedy sent 15,000 US troops to Vietnam, a country that most Americans could not find on a map. These soldiers joined forces with South Vietnamese troops in a war against the communist forces of North Vietnam. This experience became America's longest war, with over 600,000 US soldiers involved by 1967. Ironically, the war was called a police action, since Congress never officially declared war. When it ended in 1973, over 58,000 US troops had died, and America had lost its first war.

Presidential Disgrace

On August 9, 1974, Richard Nixon became the only US president to fail to finish his term (for reasons other than death) when he resigned from the office. He famously waved goodbye to the American people as he stepped aboard *Marine One*, the presidential helicopter. Nixon resigned over the Watergate scandal. This was a scandal in which members of his staff paid burglars to break into the Democratic Party headquarters office during the 1972 presidential campaign. Ironically, Nixon did not need to cheat to win that election; he won by eighteen million votes, the largest popular vote margin ever.

Two Hundred Amazing Years and Counting!

America celebrated its 200th birthday on July 4, 1976, with a year-long celebration. It seemed as if every surface in the nation was painted red, white, and blue in that year of near-continuous parades and fireworks. One highlight of the year was Operation Sail, in which sixteen tall sailing ships from around the world sailed into New York Harbor. The 200th birthday, or bicentennial, dates back to the signing of Thomas Jefferson's Declaration of Independence. The Declaration was a statement to Britain's King George III that the thirteen colonies would no longer live under his control. The Declaration was signed in the second year of the Revolutionary War. When it was signed, it was by no means certain that the colonies could win the war and become truly independent. However, as you already know, the American colonies did win, and every year a great nation celebrates its birthday on the anniversary of that great declaration.

GLOSSARY

Amphibious – A military invasion in which troops arrive by ship to attack a shore

Artillery – Any large gun or canon capable of firing projectiles long distances

Assassination – The murder of an important person, often for political reasons

Atomic bomb – A bomb vastly more powerful than a conventional bomb that creates heat by splitting radioactive atoms of uranium or plutonium

Baby boom – Post-World War II period from 1945-1964 in which fifteen million US military personnel came home, married, and started families, leading to a massive rise in the nation's birth rate

Backwoodsman – Someone who lives in a forested area away from cities

Butternut – A light yellow-brown color; the color worn by some Confederate soldiers

Caribbean – The islands and sea located to the east of Central America, including Cuba, Hispaniola, Jamaica, and the Bahamas

Cash crop – A plant grown to be sold rather than used by the people growing it

Cease-fire – A military agreement to stop fighting

Civil Rights Movement – The social movement in the United States aimed at ending discrimination against and oppression of African-Americans

Communist – Supporting or based on communism, a totalitarian system where goods and property are shared

Confederate States of America – The alliance of eleven southern states during the Civil War

Cotton diplomacy – An approach used by the Confederacy during the Civil War to win foreign support by appealing to their reliance on cotton

Depression – Period in which business and employment are at a very low level, resulting in loss of financial prosperity

Democracy – Government in which the people hold ruling power, both directly and through elected representatives

Dictator – A person with absolute power who orders others about without mercy

Gold rush – An event in which many people travel to a place to search for gold

Hispaniola – The second-largest island in the Caribbean, which is currently divided into two countries, Haiti and the Dominican Republic

Hydrogen bomb – A bomb much more powerful than an atomic bomb that imitates the sun by fusing hydrogen atoms to create intense heat

Influenza –A virus that attacks the upper respiratory system, causing fever, congestion, and muscle aches

Injustice – Unfairness; a lack of justice

Integration – Blending or mixing, such as when the US Supreme Court ordered integration of white and black students in schools in the 1950s

Massacre – The killing of a large number of people

Medal of Honor – The highest US military award given to members of the armed forces for outstanding bravery in combat beyond the call of duty

Polio – An infectious disease of the spinal cord that paralyzes its victims

Prosperity – A condition in which people's needs are met, and they experience financial good fortune

Racist – A person who mistakenly believes that one race of people is better than other races

Rebel – Nickname for a soldier of the Confederacy during the Civil War

Roaring twenties – Referring to the lively way people lived in the 1920s

Satellite – Any object, natural or man-made, that revolves around the earth or any celestial body

Secede – To leave a group, such as when some southern states left the Union before the Civil War

Segregated – Unfairly separated from others, especially referring to racial segregation

Slavery – A situation in which people are captured or owned by other people and forced to work against their will, which still exists in many places today

Stowaway – Someone who hides on a vehicle so they can travel for free and in secret

Taxation – A system by which governments collect money from citizens in order to pay for the operation of the country

Ticker-tape parade – A parade honoring a dignitary or hero, in which confetti and paper are thrown onto the streets

Torpedo – A bomb that propels through the water and strikes the side of a ship just below the water line, causing the ship to sink

Trinkets – Small objects considered valuable

U-Boat – A German submarine or underwater boat

Watershed moment – A crucial turning point affecting actions and opinions

INDEX

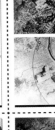
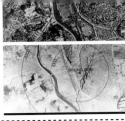